Buddhist temple

Offerings to the Buddha

Lisa Magloff

Word list

Look out for these words as you go through the book. They are shown using CAPITALS.

ALMS Donations to the poor and needy or to monks and nuns.

BODHI TREE The name given to the tree under which the Buddha sat on the night he became enlightened. The tree itself was a type of fig. In the centuries after the Buddha, the Bodhi tree became a symbol of the Buddha's presence and an object of worship.

BUDDHA The founder of Buddhism. The Buddha's name was Siddhartha Gautama and he was born in India in the 5th century BCE. The word Buddha means "enlightened one".

BUDDHISM The religion founded by the Buddha. Buddhism is not based on a belief in God or in gods. It is based on the teachings of the Buddha.

CHORTEN A Tibetan word for stupa.

DHAMMA The complete teachings of the Buddha. Also spelled dharma.

ENLIGHTENMENT The goal of Buddhists. When a person is enlightened they do not feel any fear or suffering.

MANDALA A picture which stands for the universe. Mandalas are used in Buddhist ceremonies and for meditation.

MANTRA A short sentence or phrase which Buddhists repeat as a type of worship.

MEDITATION An exercise that helps Buddhists to concentrate. There are many different ways to meditate and many non-Buddhists also meditate.

MONASTERY A very large Buddhist temple where a lot of monks or nuns live. A monastery may also contain free schools, free hospitals or other things which help the community.

MONK A Buddhist man who has given up all of his possessions and dedicated his life to studying Buddhism and helping others.

MUDRAS Hand positions that are used in Buddhist art to tell something about the Buddha.

NIRVANA The name that the Buddha gave to the goal of Buddhism. When a person has achieved nirvana, they are free from suffering, hate and greed.

NUN A Buddhist woman who has given up all of her possessions and dedicated her life to studying Buddhism and helping others.

OFFERINGS Gifts that are used to thank the Buddha for his teachings. Common offerings are incense, water, flowers and fruit. Good thoughts can also be an offering. Each type of offering helps worshippers to remember important things about the Buddha's teachings.

PAGODA A word used in China, Japan and Korea for a stupa. Pagodas are usually shaped like a tower with five levels and many have very beautiful roofs with upturned corners.

PALI A written form of Sanskrit. Many Buddhist holy books are written in Pali.

PARINIRVANA POSE In this pose, the Buddha is lying on his side. This reminds worshippers of the Buddha's death, when he lay on his side and died very peacefully.

POSE The position of the Buddha in statues and paintings. Each pose reminds Buddhists of one of the Buddha's teachings or of an event in his life.

PUJA A type of Buddhist worship where worshippers may chant mantras, ring bells and say prayers that help them to remember the Buddha's teachings and to thank the Buddha.

SANGHA The worldwide community of Buddhist monks and nuns.

SANSKRIT An ancient language used by the Buddha.

SHRINE A platform with a statue or painting of the Buddha which is the focus of worship.

SHRINE ROOM A room or building where worship takes place.

STUPA A type of building which reminds Buddhists of the burial mounds that the Buddha's ashes were placed in.

THANGKA A type of Buddhist painting which shows one or more of the Buddha's teachings.

TIPITAKA A Buddhist holy book containing the Buddha's teachings and the teachings of important Buddhists who lived after the Buddha. The Tipitaka is written in a language called Pali and so is sometimes called the Pali Canon.

Contents

 Be considerate!

When visiting a place of worship, remember that it is sacred to believers and so be considerate to their feelings. It doesn't take a lot of effort – just attitude.

Lighting incense sticks

What is a Buddhist temple for?

A Buddhist temple is a place to learn about and thank the Buddha.

BUDDHISM is an ancient religion which is practised throughout the world. It was founded by a man named Siddhartha Gautama, who lived in India 2,500 years ago. Siddhartha Gautama is also called the **BUDDHA,** and a Buddhist is a person who follows his teachings.

The temple

A Buddhist temple is a place where Buddhists go to worship. Buddhists do not pray to God when they worship. Instead, Buddhists worship by thinking about and learning the lessons that the Buddha taught, and by thanking the Buddha for his teachings.

Worship in the temple

Many of the things you will find in and around a Buddhist temple are used in Buddhist worship. Some of them are used to remind people of the lessons the Buddha taught, or to help people learn more about Buddhism and the Buddha (pictures ① and ②). Others help worshippers to thank the Buddha for his teachings.

Bird-like decorations called chofahs

Nagas

◄▲ ① The decorations on these temples are called nagas, which means serpent, and chofahs, which look like bird heads. Many Buddhist temples in South East Asia have nagas as decoration. They are an ancient symbol of protection. On temples, the nagas are thought to guard against evil.

The Buddha's teachings

The Buddha's teachings are based on the idea that suffering and unhappiness is caused by people being selfish and greedy (picture ③).

The Buddha taught that if people are not selfish or greedy then they will become truly happy and at peace with the world. In Buddhism, this is called ENLIGHTENMENT.

The Four Noble Truths

When the Buddha first began to teach people how to become enlightened, his first teachings were:

❶ That there is suffering and unhappiness in the world.
❷ Suffering is caused by greed and hatred.
❸ It is possible to end suffering and unhappiness.
❹ You can end suffering by following the lessons of the Eightfold Path.

The Eightfold Path

The Buddha taught that by living according to these eight rules, people would be happier:

❶ Right Understanding: Understand the lessons of Buddhism.
❷ Right Attitude: Do not be greedy or angry.
❸ Right speech: Avoid lying, gossip, hate speech and tale-telling.
❹ Right Action: Do not steal, cheat or kill.
❺ Right Livelihood: Make your living in an honest way that does not harm others.
❻ Right Effort: Do your best to be a good person.
❼ Right Mindfulness: Be aware and attentive.
❽ Right Concentration: If you make your mind steady and calm you will be able to become enlightened.

Buddhist words

Many of the words used by Buddhists are in an ancient language called SANSKRIT, which was the language spoken by the Buddha. For example, the word Buddha is a Sanskrit word which means "Enlightened One". The Sanskrit word for the teachings of the Buddha is DHAMMA. Some Buddhist holy books are also written in Sanskrit or in a form of Sanskrit called PALI.

In the following pages we will learn more about what is inside the Buddhist temple and how the temple is used to help people become enlightened.

▶ ② Buddhist temples always have statues of the Buddha. Buddhists do not worship these statues. Instead, the statues help people remember the Buddha and his lessons.

◀ ③ The most important of the lessons that the Buddha taught are called the Four Noble Truths and the Eightfold Path. Together, these lessons are called the Wheel of Law. Buddhists believe that by following these lessons they can become enlightened.

Weblink: www.CurriculumVisions.com

A Buddhist temple

Large Buddhist temples often have many buildings. Some are used for worship and others for living in.

Picture ① shows a large Buddhist temple. It has many features.

Central shrine

In the centre of the temple is the **SHRINE ROOM**. It contains a statue or painting of the Buddha. The shrine room is where people worship in groups or alone.

In many large temples, like this one, the main shrine room is a building in the middle of the temple. There may also be other, smaller shrine rooms in the temple, as well as statues and paintings of the Buddha both inside and outside the temple.

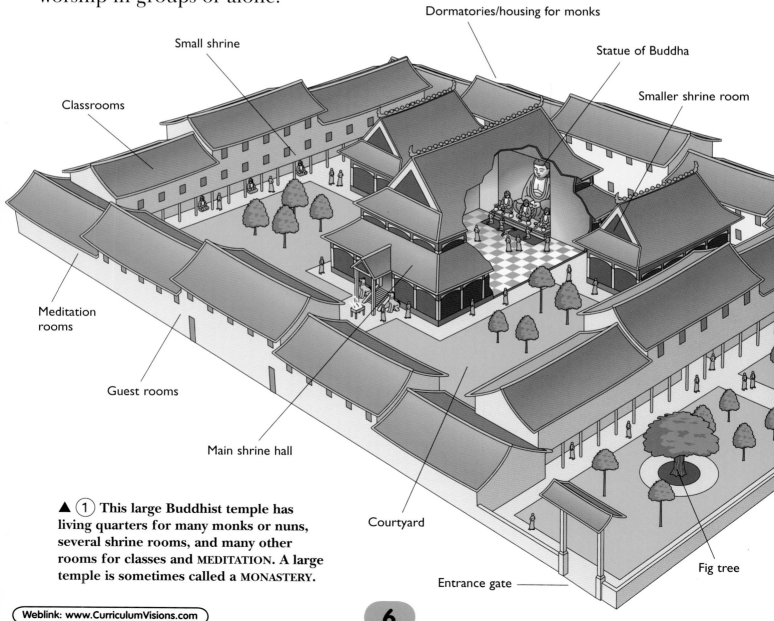

Dormatories/housing for monks

Small shrine

Statue of Buddha

Classrooms

Smaller shrine room

Meditation rooms

Guest rooms

Main shrine hall

Courtyard

Fig tree

Entrance gate

▲ ① **This large Buddhist temple has living quarters for many monks or nuns, several shrine rooms, and many other rooms for classes and MEDITATION. A large temple is sometimes called a MONASTERY.**

Stupas and pagodas

In some temples, you will see a tower called a **STUPA**, a **PAGODA** or a **CHORTEN** (picture ②).

Stupas and chortens are shaped like a dome with a tower on top. They have five parts: steps, dome, stone railing, pinnacle and peak. Inside are statues of the Buddha or of other important Buddhist teachers. Pagodas are shaped like tall towers, but they also have five levels.

A place to live

Large Buddhist temples may have people living in them. These people might be **MONKS** (men) or **NUNS** (women).

Pagoda

People who are not monks or nuns may also stay at the temple for a few days or weeks in order to study Buddhism.

Courtyard

Many large temples have one or more courtyards. These are places where monks and nuns can gather to talk, or where festivals may be held. The courtyard, and any plants and trees, also helps the monastery to feel peaceful and calm so the people who live and visit there can also feel calm and at peace.

Trees for enlightenment

One day the Buddha was sitting under a fig tree. Suddenly, he realised how to be free from suffering and fear, or enlightened. The tree the Buddha sat under was named the **BODHI TREE**, or enlightenment tree. Some monasteries have fig trees planted in their courtyards to remind people of the time when the Buddha became enlightened.

◀ ② **In different countries, pagodas have different shapes and are called different names. For example, a pagoda is often called a chorten in Tibet, a dagoba in Sri Lanka, a stupa in India, a prang in Cambodia, a that in Laos and a tap in Korea.**

This pagoda is in Thailand and is known as a chedi – Phra Sri Ratana Chedi. This chedi is said to have the remains of the Buddha's breastbone underneath it.

The shrine room

Buddhist temples come in many different styles, but most of them are very simple inside.

The **SHRINE ROOM** is the focal point of worship in the temple. There are usually no chairs in the shrine room (pictures ① and ②). This is because people sit on the floor or on cushions when they worship.

▲ ① The shrine room. (Inset) The bowls of saffron coloured water, flowers, candles and incense are offerings used to thank the Buddha.

▲ ② This smaller shrine room has a wall hanging showing the Buddha as well as smaller statues. Note the photographs on the wall and mantlepiece.

The shrine

The shrine room always contains a statue or painting of the Buddha. This is raised on a platform or a shelf to remind people that the Buddha was important. The platform with a statue on it is called a **SHRINE** (picture ①).

People often place things like flowers, water, incense and candles (picture ① inset), called **OFFERINGS**, around the statue of the Buddha. Leaving offerings is a way of showing respect for the Buddha.

Offerings

Each type of offering reminds people of different things the Buddha taught.

Candles, for example, give out the light that stands for wisdom. Light reminds people that the light of knowledge and learning sends away the darkness of ignorance.

Water stands for calmness, clarity and purity. It reminds people to clear their minds of bad thoughts and ignorance.

Incense is burned because its fragrance spreads and reminds people that good thoughts also spread.

Fruit and flowers remind people that nothing lasts forever and they should value what they have now.

In addition to these traditional offerings, there might also be objects, such as photographs of important Buddhist teachers (picture ②), or books containing the Buddha's teachings, on the shrine.

A peaceful place

It is very important that the shrine room be a quiet and peaceful place. So it is always kept clean and tidy, and there are usually no bright lights or loud noises in the shrine room.

Weblink: www.CurriculumVisions.com

Statues of the Buddha

The statue of the Buddha is the most important part of the temple.

The statues and pictures of the Buddha are the most important parts of the temple. In ancient times, statues and paintings of the Buddha were used to help teach people about Buddha's life and teachings. In these artworks, the position of the Buddha and the positions of the hands stand for different teachings or particular parts of Buddha's life.

Special positions

In statues and paintings, the Buddha is often shown in one of four **POSES**, called asanas. Each asana has a special meaning and reminds Buddhists of different events in the Buddha's life.

For example, if the Buddha is shown lying on his right side, this is called the **PARINIRVANA POSE** (see page 22). This reminds worshippers of the day the Buddha died, when he lay on his right side.

The position of the Buddha's hands, called **MUDRAS**, also have important meanings (picture ①). For example, when the Buddha's right hand is raised, this means "have no fear".

▲▶ ① The Buddha's thumb and forefinger are making a circle, like a wheel. This reminds Buddhists of the Buddha's first sermon, when he described the most basic principle of Buddhism, called the Wheel of Law (see page 5, picture ③).

One of the most common mudras is called bhumisparsa, or earth-witness (picture ②). This position reminds Buddhists of the time the Buddha was meditating and was tempted by evil. The Buddha touched his hand to the ground and asked the earth to witness that he would not be tempted.

Peaceful and calm

If you look at statues or paintings of the Buddha, you will notice that he always looks very peaceful and calm, never upset or angry.

► ② This statue of the Buddha is in the lotus pose. This is the traditional pose of meditation. The hands are in the earth-witness, or bhumisparsa mudra.

▲ ③ This worshipper is placing gold leaf on a statue of the Buddha as an offering.

Buddhists believe that being calm helps them to become enlightened. When they look at a statue of the Buddha, they are reminded of this.

Many statues

Buddhists also believe that making a statue or a painting of the Buddha is a type of worship. So, in a temple there may be hundreds of statues of the Buddha (see page 23). Or, there may be huge statues made out of stone or covered in gold (picture ③). When people clean these statues or help to build them, they believe they are helping themselves to become enlightened.

Worship in the shrine room

Different types of worship take place in the shrine room.

Not all Buddhists worship in the same way. For example, people from Tibet sometimes spin prayer wheels as a kind of worship. Other people may worship by walking around the statue of the Buddha, bowing (picture ①) or lighting incense sticks or candles as offerings. However, most kinds of Buddhist worship includes prayer, chanting and meditation.

Prayers

One type of worship in a Buddhist temple is a type of group worship called **PUJA**. Puja may be led by a monk or nun. It usually includes chanting the Five Precepts, or guidelines (picture ②). These are: do not harm living things; do not act badly; do not take what has not been given; do not lie or say bad things about other people; and do not use drugs or alcohol.

▼ ① **Many Buddhists will bow three times in front of the statue of the Buddha. The three bows stand for the Three Jewels of Buddhism: the Buddha, the teachings of the Buddha, and the worldwide community of Buddhist monks and nuns.**

▼ ② These people are worshipping by chanting the Five Precepts.

This bronze bell is a symbol of wisdom

This bronze thunderbolt, or varja, is a symbol of compassion

A prayer book containing mantras

◄ ③ Items used in Buddhist puja. The prayer beads (bottom right), also called malas, are used to count the number of mantras said during worship.

Puja might also include **MANTRAS**. These are short, simple sentences that are chanted over and over.

Buddhist puja may also include thinking about different lessons that the Buddha taught, chanting prayers that thank the Buddha, making offerings, singing, ringing bells and using prayer beads (picture ③)

A special kind of exercise

A Buddhist temple is also a place for people to practise a type of exercise called **MEDITATION** (picture ④).

In meditation, people sit quietly and try to make their mind calm and peaceful. They try to empty their minds of bad or unhappy thoughts.

Another way that Buddhists worship is by learning about Buddhism.

◄ ④ Meditation teaches people to concentrate and pay attention, so they can be calm and care about others no matter what is happening around them.

Art and symbols in the temple

Buddhist temples are filled with art and symbols that have important meaning for Buddhists.

When Buddhism began, very few people could read. So, Buddhists in different countries began using paintings and sculptures to help people learn and remember important things about the Buddha and his teachings. All of the paintings and sculptures in a Buddhist temple have important meaning.

Thangkas and mandalas

Special paintings in the temple are called **THANGKAS** and **MANDALAS** (pictures ① and ②).

▼ ① Many Buddhist paintings show lions. The lion stands for power, strength and royalty.

► ② This thangka shows Tara, an enlightened woman who stands for compassion and protection. She sits on a lotus flower.

Buddha

Many thangkas and mandala paintings show the Buddha. Some of them tell stories of the Buddha's life. Other paintings help people to remember the Buddha's teachings.

The Wheel of Life

This type of mandala painting shows a wheel, and inside it are six sections showing different kinds of people, different stages of life and different evils. Sometimes, there are paintings of a wheel with eight spokes (picture ③). This wheel stands for the Eightfold Path (see page 5).

▲ ③ This painting of a wheel is called the Wheel of Law.

▶ ④ The lotus stands for purity because the beautiful flowers grow up out of the mud. So, the lotus also stands for each person's ability to rise out of bad or ugly situations and be good.

Everything in the paintings has a special meaning, even the colours. For example, red stands for compassion, blue stands for truth and white stands for purity.

Sometimes Buddhists might look at the pictures while they meditate and this helps them to think about the Buddha's teachings. Painting the thangkas and mandalas is also sometimes a type of worship. While they paint, the artist might recite prayers and think about the Buddha's teachings.

Lotus flower

Many Buddhist paintings have a picture of a lotus flower in them (pictures ② and ④). Seeing a lotus flower reminds people that anyone can become enlightened.

Paintings and statues of the Buddha often show him sitting or standing on a lotus flower, or on a throne made of lotus petals. People sometimes also use live lotus flowers as offerings at shrines.

Celebrating at the temple

The temple is where the Buddhist community comes together for celebrations and festivals.

Throughout the year, many celebrations and festivals are held in Buddhist temples. Many of these festivals celebrate important events in the life of the Buddha or other important Buddhist teachers.

Buddhist festivals are always joyous and happy occasions (picture ①).

▼ ① Traditional Thai dancing at a Thai Buddhist festival.

Usually, people will go to a local temple and offer food and drink to the monks and nuns. They may also worship with the monks and nuns, eat special food, listen to talks, watch dances, sing and give donations (picture ②).

Buddha Day

The most important holiday is Buddha Day, or Vesak. This holiday celebrates the day the Buddha was born, the day the Buddha became enlightened and the day the Buddha died. These events all happened on the same day in different years.

▲ ② This family is making a donation to the temple during a festival. They are bowing to receive the blessing of a monk.

▼ ③ These women are lighting candles as an offering to the Buddha during a festival.

To celebrate this day, Buddhists decorate their houses and make offerings at the temple. One important part of this festival is lighting candles (picture ③) and lights in the temples and at home. These stand for the enlightenment of the Buddha.

Songkran

Some Buddhist festivals are celebrated only in a particular country. For example, the festival of Songkran is celebrated by Thai Buddhists in the middle of April. People gather around the riverbank, carrying live fish in jars to put in the water. April is very hot in Thailand and the ponds dry out. So the fish would die if they were not rescued. This reminds Buddhists of the importance of caring for others – even fish. People also splash the monks and each other with water and have boat races.

Another festival, the Festival of the Tooth, is only celebrated in the town of Kandy in Sri Lanka. In this town there is a temple that houses one of the teeth of the Buddha. Once a year the tooth is taken out and paraded around town on elephant-back.

Lunar festivals

Many Buddhist festivals take place when there is a full moon. For example, in Thailand, Burma, Sri Lanka, Cambodia and Laos, the Buddhist New Year starts on the first full moon in April.

Visiting a Buddhist temple

The best way to learn about a Buddhist temple is to visit one. Before you visit, you should know something about what you will see and do.

In most Buddhist temples, anyone is welcome at any time – you do not have to be a Buddhist. In fact, many people go to Buddhist temples just to have a place to be quiet and calm.

What will we see and do in the shrine room?

Before you enter the shrine room, you will have to take off your shoes (picture ①). This keeps the shrine room clean and also shows respect for the Buddha.

It is important to remember that many Buddhists come to the temple in order to worship quietly by themselves, so you should always be quiet and show respect when you are in the temple.

Remember that around the temple there may be many objects, paintings or sculptures to remind Buddhists of the teachings of the Buddha. For example, you may see thangkas or mandalas.

▼▶ ① **Praying in front of Buddha in a shrine room. Note the bare feet. (Inset) People entering the temple take their shoes off.**

You may also see specially-shaped books containing copies of the teachings of the Buddha. These books are called the **TIPITAKA** (picture ②) and they may be written in **SANSKRIT** or another language. You may want to ask the person showing you around if you can see the writing.

▲ ② The tipitaka, which means "the three baskets", contains the teachings of the Buddha.

What will you see and do outside the shrine room?

Outside the shrine room, there may be a prayer wheel (picture ③). On the outside and inside of the prayer wheel are the words:

Om Mani Padme Om

This is a prayer which means "All hail the jewel in the lotus". The jewel in the lotus is another name for the Buddha.

You will not be participating in worship, but you may see Buddhists leaving offerings or bowing in front of the statue of the Buddha or they may place the palms of their hands together and raise them to their chin or chest.

You may be shown around the temple by a monk or a nun. These are people who live at the temple and have dedicated their lives to studying and practising the teachings of the Buddha. You can learn more about monks and nuns on the following pages.

▼ ③ Many people believe that every time a prayer wheel spins around it is the same as saying a prayer. You do not have to be a Buddhist to spin a prayer wheel.

Weblink: www.CurriculumVisions.com

Living at the temple

Some Buddhists choose to dedicate their lives to studying Buddhism. These are Buddhist monks and nuns.

People who have decided to dedicate their lives to studying the teachings of the Buddha are called **MONKS** (if they are men) and **NUNS** (if they are women). The word for the worldwide community of Buddhist monks and nuns is **SANGHA**.

A way of life

Buddhist monks and nuns give up all of their possessions and live away from their families in a temple or **MONASTERY** (see pages 6 to 7). Everything that they eat or use is given to them by other Buddhists. These donations are called **ALMS**. Buddhists believe that giving alms to monks and nuns is one way to become a better person.

The monks and nuns spend their lives studying and teaching the lessons of the Buddha. They also help in the running of the temple.

There are many rules which monks and nuns must follow, such as only eating one meal a day, not sleeping on a soft bed, and following the Five Precepts (five guidelines).

▼ ① Young men often become monks for just a short time.

A temporary way of life

In some Buddhist countries, parents might send their children to a temple to be monks or nuns for only a few months or a few years (picture ①). In the monastery, children are taught about Buddhism, as well as the usual school subjects (picture ③).

Helping the community

In some countries, the monastery also provides counselling, free schooling, free medical clinics, orphanages, and other things that people need.

▶ ② The robe is always a very simple piece of cloth with no buttons or zip.

▶ ③ A monk teaches the lessons of the Buddha.

If a monk or a nun has a skill, such as carpentry, then they will still use that skill once they have become a monk or nun. But instead of using the skill to make money for themselves, they will use it to help the monastery and to help others in the community, such as helping to build houses for the poor.

Robes

Buddhist monks and nuns usually wear special robes. These are similar to those the Buddha wore. There are many different styles and colour of robe (pictures ① and ②).

Buddhist temples in Thailand

There are many different styles of Buddhist temple around the world. Here you can see what temples look like in Thailand.

Buddhism, and Buddhist temples, are not exactly the same all over the world. As a result, in each country there are local styles of building.

Buddhist temples are among the world's most beautiful buildings. Here we give you a glimpse of what Thai temples are like.

Temples of Bangkok

The capital city of Thailand is Bangkok. In this city there are some of the most impressive temples in Thailand.

Occupying a 20-hectare site next to the Royal Grand Palace, Wat Pho is the oldest and largest temple in Bangkok. It was built in 1688 during the reign of King Petraja of Ayutthaya and contains one of Thailand's most spectacular sights, a 46-metre long and 15-metre high statue of a reclining Buddha (picture ①). The gold-plated statue has mother-of-pearl on the soles of the feet (picture ②), and was not added until 1832 during the reign of King Rama III.

◀ ① **This posture is called the PARINIRVANA POSE. It shows the Buddha lying on his side, just before his death and his passing into NIRVANA (the state of absolute blessedness).**

▼ ② **The mother-of-pearl design on the soles of the reclining Buddha's feet show 108 symbols of good luck, arranged in 67 small squares around the circle, or chakra, at the centre of each foot.**

▼ ③ One of the demon guardians at the Royal Grand Palace.

▲ ④ Some of the many Buddha statues at Wat Pho.

The grounds of Wat Pho house over 1,000 Buddha statues (picture ④), the largest such collection in Thailand, as well as 95 stupas – Buddhist religious monuments – and a series of marble slabs depicting part of the epic Thai poem, the Ramakian, which tells of the struggle between good and evil. The palace is guarded by statues of demon-like creatures (picture ③). Visitors can also wander amongst the peaceful rock gardens and chapels. King Rama III also established Wat Pho as an important centre for Thai medicine and massage and thus founded Thailand's oldest seat of learning.

Index

Curriculum Visions is a registered trademark of
Atlantic Europe Publishing Company Ltd.

◈ *Atlantic Europe Publishing*

Teacher's Guide
There is a Teacher's Guide to accompany this
book, available only from the publisher.

Dedicated Web Site
There's more about other great Curriculum
Visions packs and a wealth of supporting
information available at our dedicated web site:

www.CurriculumVisions.com

First published in 2005 by
Atlantic Europe Publishing Company Ltd
Copyright © 2005
Atlantic Europe Publishing Company Ltd

All rights reserved. No part of this
publication may be reproduced, stored in a
retrieval system, or transmitted in any form
or by any means, electronic, mechanical,
photocopying, recording or otherwise,
without prior permission of the Publisher.

Authors
Lisa Magloff, MA and Brian Knapp, BSc, PhD

Religious Adviser
John Underwood

Art Director
Duncan McCrae, BSc

Senior Designer
Adele Humphries, BA

Acknowledgements
The publishers would like to thank the
following for their help and advice:
The Buddhapadipa Temple, Wimbledon
and Jamyang Buddhist Centre, London.

Photographs
The Earthscape Editions photolibrary.

Illustrations
David Woodroffe

Designed and produced by
Earthscape Editions

Printed in China by
WKT Company Ltd

Buddhist temple – *Curriculum Visions*
A CIP record for this book is
available from the British Library

Paperback ISBN 1 86214 420 6
Hardback ISBN 1 86214 422 2

*This product is manufactured from
sustainable managed forests. For every tree
cut down at least one more is planted.*